BECAUSE I'M HAPPY

A Key to Change

LB DUTCHESS

7 Publishing

ISBN-13: 978-0692589519
ISBN-10: 0692589511

Book Cover Design by Saba Tekle

Acknowledgments

This has been one of many topics I have been working on for the last 15 years. And thanks to my hubby, Brett, for being antagonistic enough to push me so I finally finish one! If it were not for him, my friends, and my family who kept telling me I could do it, this might still be just notes on my iPhone.

iv

Content

Chapter 1
~ It's a matter of perspective ~

Do you fight the basics of life?

I hear people talking all the time, and by default, focusing on the things that make them unhappy. I find it is usually because they have an unreal expectation of what life has to offer. So, let's take a moment to put things into perspective. Let's go back to basics.

When we are born, the *jump-start* to our life is usually some sort of a dramatic entrance into this world. We come from a very confined, rhythmic, and provided-for situation to one of intense light, sound, and the demands of our heart to start pumping blood through our veins and our lungs laboring to breathe. From the moment we are born, our body is in some state of labor – never stopping or the body ceases to function, and we die. Too many minutes without oxygen? You're dead. Your heart stops pumping? You're dead. So, what does your body do? It finds a rhythm and goes with it. Your heart and lungs find a pace that creates a sense of peace in pumping the blood, bringing the oxygen in, and getting everything you need where it needs to go... second by second, minute by minute. The labor is necessary, so the body just goes with it – no questions asked.

Now riddle me this... What if you applied this principle to your life? What if you took on the mindset that if your body has to labor for EVERY breath it takes and EVERY beat of your heart JUST to survive and it does this your ENTIRE life with little complaint, don't you think you can too? Why would you think anything in life should be any easier? If you realize that life is a labor and it's only a matter of finding your rhythm, you can change your state of mind. You can find your Happy.

Let's go a step further. Does your heart decide some days that *I don't want to work so hard, so I think I will take some short cuts and only pump blood through some of the veins*? Does it say *I don't want to pump today. I'm not happy about this pumping thing I have to do day in and day out*? How effective do you think that would be for your body? Or, how about your lungs deciding that they want a 20-minute break? Well, we usually call that dead. And if you are of the mindset of looking only for the short cuts to the basics in life, you will find yourself in a near-death state for as long as you choose to remain focused on those shortcuts. Life is about rhythm and purpose and balance, and these equal happiness. So, find your rhythm in what you must do to survive, define your purpose so you know why you are doing things, and create a balance with the things in life that you want to do while taking care of the things in life that you need. Then, you will find some happiness in your daily life. Don't make the basics of life a conscript to happiness; your happiness in the basics is irrelevant. Find your happiness while doing the basics as well as outside of the basics!

Chapter 2
~ Happiness as a concept ~

Do you choose your own destiny?

Each of us is responsible for our own happiness. Granted, when we are small, that happiness is governed in part by those who raise us. BUT, we have a choice in how we deal with our moments to ourselves, even in the greatest of struggles. Keeping your wits about you is not just the stuff of actions films; it is a key to a productive and happy life – like controlling where your thoughts go and realizing what you are forming opinions about and whether those opinions are relevant to your life. Are you protecting what you fill your mind with from outside sources? These are the things you have the most control over. So use that control, wield it like the power of a super-hero, and defend your mind from the unnecessary and harmful influences!

You have probably heard some of the great one-liners of movie history – "You may take this body, but it will not be me... It will NOT be me," screamed Lady Marian as the sheriff of Nottingham prepared to take his privilege of forcing her marriage; or in Braveheart starring Mel Gibson, when they are quartering him and he chooses his final moments to scream, "FREEDOM," instead of saying what they want him to and admitting to a lie. These are prime examples of making choices on how we are going to let life have an impact on us, even in the most desperate of situations. We do have choices...maybe not in what we are dealing with but rather how we choose to deal with it and how we choose to let it affect us and our future choices. It can be the difference between being a success or a victim. The concept of being happy is our own decision.

So how does this apply to you in your everyday, simple existence of life? Well, let's take a look at your job. Let's just say for this argument's sake that you have a job that you didn't dream of as a kid. Somehow, your choices and life brought you to a place where you now go to a job every day that does not excite you. More depressingly, maybe it doesn't even pay all of your bills. Day in and day out, you find yourself feeling more and more trapped and getting more and more frustrated with where you are. This point is where most people go terribly awry. However, this is where you hold some of your greatest power. So, ST-OP... Take a deep breath... And look to find SOMETHING to be thankful for in this job that is less than what you want. Breathe, and focus on everything and anything positive you can find in your job. Change how you look at it. Work to bring a smile to your face as often as you can throughout the day by minding what you are allowing your brain to think, and you will start to see a change – a change in how others look at you; a change in how YOU look at you. Opportunities will begin to present themselves. You will attract those opportunities because there is nothing like a positive outlook to give and send out positive energy, which in turn motivates you. You will take control of your future in a way that no one but you has the power to take away, and that is because the only way it can be taken away is if you give it up. So, choose not to give up your positive and thankful attitude, and keep an eager eye out for opportunities to present themselves!

Chapter 3
~ A Definition of Happy ~

What is Happiness?

While the specifics are different for all of us, the semantics for us are all about the same. Happiness is...

1. *An Action that must be pursued daily* – It is our choice to focus on the things around us that make us happy while working on fixing or adjusting the things that do not make us happy. It is an action that must be started by YOU each and every day and worked out like a muscle.

2. *A state of mind that must be chosen.* While it is true that we cannot control all the things that go on

around us or that happen to us, we can choose how we respond to them and how much time, energy, and emotion we allot to our environment.

3. *Defined by you.* Each of us has different things that make us happy. Some people are happy with friends and family around them. Some are happy with financial stability, and some are happy when they're surrounded in nature and in solitude. These are just some of the ways we all find happiness. You must first identify what makes you happy, and then find ways to accommodate your daily life to include these things so that your journey is less daunting. Let's face it, life is a struggle no matter what life you're living.

Chapter 4
~ Finding your new "Happy" ~

Can you start your journey?

So, if you feel you have struggled in finding happiness or that you have never really been happy, how do you find your Happy?

We will start with the basic approach. Walk out your front door. Take a walk around where you live. Look at the life happening around you 10 to 1,000 feet from where you live. Look for the smiles on people's faces. What are they doing? Why are they smiling?

Look up to the sky... Is it clear, blue, and peaceful; magnificent in its awesomeness? Are clouds floating across the sky overhead traveling across miles and miles of land? Is the sky raining and providing vital water to the plants and the waterways around that sustain you? How does this make you feel? What is it that you see in your immediate environment?

Look at this like treasure hunting. These moments of happiness going on around you are dazzling gems. They are strong, illuminating, and stand out. Let your mind capture these gems and string them together to form jewels that you can keep with you through all the troubles of your daily life until you can find your own gems to replace them.

Now, go where you can look down on the area you live in, like a roof top or perhaps a hill. Displace yourself from the immediate hustle and bustle of survival, and watch as life perpetually moves forward…

Regardless of how we choose to interact with it, life will still move forward. Children will still be born; people will still eat and celebrate; and we will still eventually pass on from this world, but it will continue moving on. People will still be happy. How are you going to choose to be a part of this life?

Go to a river or stream. Place a leaf on the water and watch what happens. If it can remain balanced on the surface, it will flow with the water where ever it takes it – intact and moving. If something causes it to fight the water, it will sink or be thrown to shore. Fortunately, we are not as helpless as the leaf most of the time, but it does provide a very basic look at life.

Now, think about what you have seen, and as you continue, make notes on what makes you smile. What lightens your heart? What inspires you? Write down some of the things you would like to do that make you happy, and plan on how to make them happen in between the basics of your life. Own every moment of happiness where you interact with the world. Smile and hold on to it as you move forward and start looking for the next smile…Your next gem.

Now, let's be clear. Doping yourself up with drugs and alcohol, numbing the pain, and removing the feelings of life will not bring you happiness. That, my friends, is called avoidance and rarely leads to happiness. Choose to deal with the things you must and focus on the things that make you happy.

Although, I must admit that I find quite a bit of

happiness in a glass or two of one of my favorite wines... :)

Chapter 5
~ Happy ~ A college course ~

Do you search for your answers?

Now that we have some basic ideas of how to start, we have to look more in depth at what the wrong kind of thoughts are that lead us away from our Happy. Our culture has made a pastime of focusing on all the wrong things, and we, by default, find ourselves confused and unhappy. Be aware of some of the following, and if you find yourself thinking like any of these, fix it.

1. *I don't know* is your answer and stopping point. Our culture has adopted *I don't know* as an actual answer to questions, but it was never meant to be! The phrase "I don't know" has been taken out of context and shortened to become the leading road to failure that it is today. What IS the entire

phrase you might ask? "I don't know, but let me find out." The phrase itself was meant to make those we were interacting with aware that our life had not yet put us in contact with that particular experience, thus we need to educate ourselves on the next course of action. We need to take responsibility moving forward! We need to go in search of our answers.

Can you imagine if Christopher Columbus, when asked if he could get to the new world, had replied, "I don't know," and left it at that?! Or, if Ben Franklin, when asked what was going to happen when the lightning struck the kite with wire on it, had replied, "I don't know," and simply walked away because he didn't know?

"I don't know" is not the entire sentence. It is part of "I don't know yet" or "I don't know, but let's find out." The beginning phrase of "I don't know" should be looked at as the beginning of a journey, not an excuse for never starting. Only by completing the sentence will you continue to grow and move forward. You may also be amazed at how much happiness you can get from solving the riddle and finding answers yourself!

2. Spend more time living a REAL life rather than watching a fake life happen on TV. One of the

most retched things that has happened to our culture is that we have taken TV from a pleasant pastime to a mind-numbing excuse to not interact with a fulfilling yet sometimes troublesome, emotion-filled, happy, sad, good, and bad life in real time! We have allowed a fake life to desensitize us to the real hardships and consequent feelings of accomplishment that come from living and experiencing life as it comes. Now, don't get me wrong. I like watching some TV shows just as much as anyone else, but I don't let my TV time last for more hours in a day than the actual time I live my life. You need to go out and experience life to find your happiness. Otherwise, you try to feel someone else's fake life and find happiness in it. How does that make sense? It's like trying to imagine what a virtual hotdog would taste like but you had never had a real one! You need the actual experience to have a point of reference, so go out and live some life.

3. Wondering why someone else has something you don't and resenting it is such a deadly thought that it is scary! You see it every day in the extremes of people stealing and killing for something they want and don't have because they feel they are entitled to it or earned it and it was taken from them. Or there's the more subtle, inner wo-

rkings of most people when they see something they want and waste vital mind-energy judging why the person who has it doesn't deserve it, but they do. The bottom line is this, if you don't have it, you don't deserve it. And here is why; your choices. Every choice you make takes you down a path that leads you to where you find yourself at any given time. Just like the leaf on the water, if you have left yourself at the mercy of the tides of life, you will find yourself where ever you get bumped to. You need to be something stronger than a leaf on the water. You need to be like a boat with a motor and plenty of gas to get you where you want to go! Resenting others for what they have is a waste of time and shows ignorance. See the things you want, make a plan on how to get them, and keep your choices in line with that plan.

For example, do you want to go on a trip? Do you drink coffee every day? Is your morning routine to swing by your local coffee hot spot every morning and get your much deserved cup of Java? Maybe you also have one at lunch time to get you through the day. That is a choice. I know you feel you *need* it to get through the day. I get it. Nonetheless, it is a choice. So, how do you adjust this choice so that you can get the trip you want? Well, here is an idea… Take the money you buy your coffee with in the morning and make the coffee at home! Physically, take the time to do it yourself and put the cash in a jar every single day you don't spend that money, and see your trip come closer and closer to reality. You don't necessarily give up anything; you simply make a choice to adjust one thing to get something else that you want. Empower yourself to get what you want by looking at your choices – ALL of your choices – and see what options you may have so you can include new choices.

Chapter 6
~ Adjusting your state of mind for Happy~

Are you making excuses?

Just as fear and faith cannot occupy the same space at the same time, neither can looking for or focusing on a problem and solving a problem. It must be a progression not a destination. You must, of course, focus on finding the problems and then quickly move on to solving the problems. Too often, people find one problem, then another problem, and then another problem. They are so focused on the problems that they forget to create the outcome of fixing the problems and lose many happy outcomes in the process.

Here is a prime example. Problem #1: You have

to get from point A to point B, but how are you going to get from point A to point B? Problem #2: (Here is where you start to get stuck) You could take a car, but you don't have a car. You can't afford a car, so you can't take a car. You could get a ride, but your friends are all busy. They have busy lives, and you don't want to bother them and ask for a ride. So, you can't get a ride. You could walk…but you don't have time to walk. You need to get to point B right away, but you don't have the time or energy to walk. So, you can't walk; therefore, you can't get to point B. You have failed and are unhappy… BUT, it was all your own choice.

In this particular instance, you had four choices or more you made that were problem-focused, not problem-solving focused. You made choices that ultimately created your situation and your resulting unhappiness. How could you have solved some of these problems that kept you from your point B? Well, let's just see.

I don't have a car and can't afford one. This is a planning issue. If your point B's in life are going to require you to get a car, then you have to plan to work toward getting a car and not wait until you need the car and use not having one as an excuse to not being happy about not getting to point B. (Whew, that's a mouth full!) So, if you are going to need a car to get to some of your point B's in life, start planning on how to make that happen right now. Don't wait until you *need* the car.

I don't want to ask for a ride; my friends are all busy. This choice is one that many *martyrs* take, creating a victim type status of not wanting to bother people. Change how you look at it and how you handle it. You could ask for the ride in exchange for helping them with something they need AND spending time with them. We all need help with things and do better when others are working with us in many instances. We are a social race, so interaction and interdependence between us is normal. Ask for help AND give help…teeter tauter…teeter tauter.

I don't have time to walk. Well, let's just be blunt here. That is poor time management on your part. If you are constantly creating situations where everything is last minute then you have no one but yourself to blame for your ensuing unhappiness of not getting to point B. The solution would be to make the time to walk by multitasking and taking the time to get your exercise in, and as I mention in Chapter 4, look around for inspiration for happiness.

The truth is, you have to be problem-solving driven. Everything else is just an excuse, and if you *can't* make something work, don't let it make you unhappy. Just make it happen at a later time.

Chapter 7
~ I'm stuck and I can't get out ~

Are you insane?

Too often we fall into the tale of insanity. You know the one – doing the same thing over and over and over and over and over and over (multiply that by a thousand, and you get my drift) again and expecting a different result. Well, my friend, that is why it is called insanity. It's kind of like running with your shoes untied. If at some point you don't stop to tie your shoes, you can't very well get angry every time you trip and fall over them. Stop fighting the fact that you have to tie your shoes. Tie them, and move the hell on! What you're stuck on are your perceived thoughts of what should and should not be. The fact of the matter is there are just some things like gravity that you can't fight. So work around, over, or through them, and sing a happy tune while you do. Replace insanity with ingenuity, and you will not only find yourself moving forward but with results that will feed your Happy.

For instance. I want to lose weight, but I love my food and wine. It is as much a social interaction with me as it is a source of energy for my body. But, let's face it. Wine is not necessary, but I don't care. I try to exercise, but things always seem to get in the way. I try to watch what I eat, but make excuses for why I deserve that less-than-healthy choice I pop in my mouth. So, I don't lose the weight. At this point, I am clinically insane when it comes to my weight loss. I am not changing anything, so I am not getting anywhere.

I had to change my way of looking at food and working out. I had to stop thinking I *deserve* that food and start thinking I *deserve* that workout! I had to stop being insane, and change followed. Figure out what you are insane about, and become aware of it so you can start to make changes. This is within your control, and you will find that by being aware of your choices you will have the power to feed your Happy.

Chapter 8
~ Not my Monkey, Not my Circus ~

Are you caught up in the lives of everyone else around you?

Not my monkey, not my circus. I heard this from my middle child, and I had to laugh out loud at its simplicity and insight. What does it mean exactly – not my Monkey, not my circus? It is in reference to control and things happening around us that don't directly affect us. It is the reminder to *learn* to work with what you *can* and let go of what you *can't*. For instance, as I mentioned earlier, I want to lose weight. I want to be more physically fit, stronger, and have more endurance. I also LOVE my wine and food. For me, it is the center of amazing memories with family and friends, so I have a tendency to eat and drink more than I exercise.

My older sons are very athletic, due in large part to us as parents pushing them, so now they have been pushing me back. They remind me to go work out and that maybe I should not eat that cake in the freezer... (Oh, how did that get there?) They get frustrated when I complain about not fitting properly into the clothes I have.

However, one day, my middle son looked at me and said, "Not my monkey, not my circus," and walked away. I was stunned! Between laughing and comprehending what he had said, I realized that he had it right! He had become as insane as I was in my continual insistence of doing the same thing over and over, so he broke the insanity.

My weight loss, and or eating the wrong foods or not, is not his problem. He can be there to help me with workouts, go running with me, or we can do sit-ups together, but he cannot control what I eat or drink – those are my monkeys and part of my circus. He chose to let go of my circus and work with his own monkeys. It wasn't rude, mean, or dismissive. It was a wonderful realization, and one that I adopted. Take control of the monkeys in your circus, and don't be offended when those around you choose to walk away from your circus when it becomes insane! If people are walking away, you should probably be asking why. And the last thing you need to worry about are other people's monkeys and how they are running their circus. Visit their circus when you have yours under control!

Chapter 9
~ Happy and the Angry little Elf ~

Are you an angry little elf?

Again, like so many other things in life, anger and happiness cannot occupy the same space at the same time. You can either be one or the other. The amount of time you spend in either is ENTIRELY within your control.

Let's put it in another way – a more knee-jerk reaction type of way. It's like food poisoning. When you eat bad food, your body makes a judgment call to get it out as fast as possible. So, it signals your stomach to send it back the way it came in. "Throw it up," it says. Now, you're a stubborn kind of person and you don't want to throw up, so you fight it tooth and nail trying to force it to stay down. Why would you do this, seriously?! Let it go, get rid of it, and move on!

This seems to be the typical control freak way of dealing with things in our lives these days. We turn into angry little elves about the most basic of things in life by trying to change things that are set up to help us get on track faster. But, in our twisted little minds, we believe there must be a better way – a shorter and less painful way to get to our end result. So, instead of embracing and moving on, we get angry and fight the known method. And, for what – an unknown method with an unknown result that usually just fuels the fire of anger? Now, let's be clear here. I am not saying don't try to find new ways of doing things. That would be stupid. What I am saying is if you find yourself angry often, you need to do some real soul-searching and discover what you need to do to fix it because anger and happiness cannot occupy the same space at the same time. Typically, you will find your anger fueled by your resistance to doing something that was created to get you to where you want to be. By doing this, you have just decided you don't like the road.

Here is a more social example of what I mean. A kid grows up with a very simple upbringing – no extra money for much of anything. He goes to school, gets good enough grades to get to college, finishes college, and comes out with a degree. He worked hard to get that degree. Maybe he even worked nights to help pay for it. Maybe it took six years to get. But, who cares? He got the degree. Now it's time to get a job. He starts applying for jobs in the field of his degree, and why would he not? But, he doesn't get a job. Time after time, he is told no. Someone suggests he start with any job to get his feet underneath him, and he gets angry. "I earned that degree! I deserve this job now!" Well, let's just stop right there. Angry elf has made him stupid at this point. While he did in fact earn the degree, he has not earned the job. He does not deserve it, and that is that. This is where so many people find themselves and begin to stop growing. They may or may not find a job and will stay angry little elves. Many, if they find a job, will continue with their angry little elf self. Even though they have the job, they will believe they are better than that job and complain and groan each day away, feeding their angry little elf selves and leaving little or no room for happiness.

So, how do you get out of this? It's simple. Take pride in the work you have chosen to do, and work toward progressing to what you want to do.

Humble steps and humble beginnings usually have an amazing way of giving us the building blocks to having a more fulfilling and prosperous life ahead of us, if only we are willing to start somewhere. I can't promise you riches and success just because you are willing to start down a path, but if you remain focused on your goals, look for ways to educate yourself on how you can get to your goals, and find all the good things life has to offer along the way you will find a life full of more happiness than anger and eliminate the angry little elf inside!

Chapter 10
~ The Happy Repellent ~

Are you chasing Happiness away?

Few truly understand that while *misery loves company* is a fact of life, it also acts as a happiness repellant. So, here are some sure-fire pitfalls to avoid if you don't want to find yourself in that negative space:

1. *Feeling sorry for yourself* – I don't care who you are, this doesn't look attractive on ANYONE, nor is there ANYWHERE in history where feeling sorry for one's self ever got anyone where they wanted to be. End of story!

2. *No One Owes You Anything.* We are responsible for our choices. We are responsible for our lives. We are responsible for our Happy. We responsible for our state of mind. The second

you start focusing on what you don't have and look at someone else as the responsible party, you will find yourself lost in an abyss few escape. Look at every decision you make as payment for your future and efforts paid-in-full, instead of your time spent and payment due.

3. *Don't get caught up in what you don't know.* There is always a way over, around, or through something. You just need to find your path.

Revel in the journey and fight for what you want in life! Allow your passion for your goals to shine bright and instead of repelling Happiness, you will attract it!

All in all, your key to change is a result of NOT expecting someone else to make you Happy, provide for you, and/or define what your Happy is. Claim and own your own state of mind, and you will find a life fueled by YOUR Happy along your journey. You're going to travel the road anyway, so why not whistle with a smile on your face as you do!

Here's to you and finding your Happy!

About the Author

As a writer, Producer, and Host of Blog Talk Radio's "Socially Savvy", LB Dutchess has spoken, for the last four years, to how to make our social experiences and interactions better by changing how we look at our interactions and our attitudes while out socially. Currently, she is developing "Socially Savvy" into a marketing and social hub where followers can connect with their community on events and entertainment. She is also working on new writing projects. In addition, LB Dutchess enjoys her photography as a means to continually find her Happy reminders in the world around her.

BECAUSE I'M HAPPY